Soup Cleanse

*Healthy Soup Recipes To Detox Your Body
And Promote Healing*

By Susan T. Williams

This book is designed to provide information on the topic covered. The information herein is offered for informational purposes solely. It is sold with the understanding that neither the author nor the publisher is engaged in rendering legal, accounting or other professional services. If legal or other professional advice is warranted, the services of an appropriate professional should be sought.

While every effort has been made to make the information presented here as complete and accurate as possible, it may contain errors, omissions or information that was accurate as of its publication but subsequently has become outdated by marketplace or industry changes. Neither author nor publisher accepts any liability or responsibility to any person or entity with respect to any loss or damage alleged to have been caused, directly or indirectly, by the information, ideas, opinions or other content in this book.

In no way, is it legal to reproduce, duplicate, or transmit any part of this document in either electronic means or printed form. Recording of this publication is strictly prohibited and any storage of this document is not allowed unless with written permission from the publisher.

The use of any trademark within this book is for clarifying purposes only, and any trademarks referenced in this work are used are without consent, and remain the property of the respective trademark holders, who are not affiliated with the publisher or this book.

Table of Contents

CHAPTER 1

What You Need to Know about Soup Cleansing

There are so many different options to choose from when it comes to full body detoxing. With soup cleanses, juice cleanses, fasting or even over the counter pills, it can be difficult to know which method of cleansing is best for you. *Soup Cleanse: Healthy Soup Recipes to Detox Your Body and Promote Healing*, however, focuses solely on the use of healthy soups to detox your body. Why? Because we believe that cleansing the body should also entail healing the body - something that can't be done with sugary juices, lack of nutrition or questionable pills.

In the following chapters, you will learn not only about the benefits of soup cleansing, but you will also find examples of how to follow a soup cleanse and some soup recipes that you can make at home.

Soup cleanses have long played a role in establishing and maintaining full body health in cultures throughout the world. From ancient Chinese healing soups to the guild apothecary soup cures of England, soups have had a significant healing role for hundreds of years. In this chapter, we will not only take a look at a brief history of soup cleansing, but we will also cover what you need to know about soup cleansing in modern times.

What is a Soup Cleanse?

In order to understand the role that soup cleansing can have on detoxifying the body, it is important to first understand what soup cleansing is. The basic principle of a soup cleanse is to detoxify the body of toxins and promote healing by ingesting soups made of whole foods and simple ingredients. These soups are specifically designed utilizing ingredients that are known for their healing properties. These properties include reduction of inflammation, neutralization of acids, inhibition of infection and improvement of digestion. The average soup cleanse may be a single day, three days or five days in length.

The soups that are best for you to cleanse with depends upon the health concerns that are being addressed. For example, someone with arthritis would focus on detoxifying soups that are made from ingredients that target inflammation as well as reduce pain. One of the best things about a soup cleanse diet, however, is that all cleansing soups provide general body detox by offering optimal nutrition.

While soup cleanse plans target specific health concerns, they also provide nutrient rich ingredients. These ingredients come without the hindrance of artificial ingredients or overly salty preservatives. This makes them more available to your body as fuel through rapid absorption. With less energy spent on breaking down food, your body can focus on healing itself by making optimal use of the natural ingredients being provided to it.

You may be asking yourself – "Aren't soup cleanses for dieters?" Well, yes…and no. Soup cleanses can offer weight loss benefits, but these benefits come from eating healthier whole foods that nourish your body. Without refined sugars, fatty foods and toxic additives, your body is much less likely to pack on excess pounds!

The History of Soup Cleansing

While soup cleansing is coming in to the spotlight these days, it is important to remember that this type of detoxifying plan has been around for hundreds of years. Of course, soup cleansing was not called "soup cleansing" back in its earlier days, rather it was a dry mixture of medicinal ingredients offered by local apothecaries or medicine men that was to be mixed with hot water to create soup with the intent of addressing specific ailments.

Depending upon the culture examined, the types of cleansing soup ingredients that were used varied. The main difference between these earlier soup cleansing methods and those being used today, however, is that today we tend to target general detox as well as specific health concerns. Throughout its earlier history, soup cleanses were used to target specific health concerns and organs, for example fevers, diarrhea and even mental health imbalances.

CHAPTER 2

One Day Soup Cleanse Menu

What Does A One Day Soup Cleanse Look Like?

The "average day" on a one day soup cleanse will obviously vary depending upon the aim of your cleansing period. For the sake of this example, we are going to assume that you simply want to detoxify your body of the various toxins we expose ourselves to everyday. These toxins are present not only in the foods that we eat, but also in the world around us, so this type of cleanse can be beneficial to just about everybody!

Below you will find a one day soup cleanse menu. You can try your first cleanse on a weekend day to see how your body reacts to it. At the end of the day and in the days following, you will feel lighter, be more regular, and you may even acquire a certain glow to your skin!

Morning

Berry Breakfast Soup

This sweet soup combines your favorite fruits with kefir, maple syrup and chili powder for a great morning wake up soup! If you are used to a sweet breakfast snack, this is the perfect soup cleanse substitute.

Super fruit blueberry offers antioxidants galore while reducing cholesterol and protecting against heart disease.

Servings: 3

Ingredients:

2 ½ cups fresh blueberries

2 ½ cups fresh strawberries

½ cup kefir

Zest and juice of one lime

1 tsp chili powder

1 tbsp maple syrup

Method:

Begin by bringing a pot of water to a simmer. Add in the blueberries and strawberries, and allow them to simmer for 10 minutes.

Once your strawberries are soft, add them to a blender with the lime juice, kefir, lime zest, maple syrup and chili powder. Blend on puree until smooth, and serve.

Mid-Morning Soup

Vegan Hot and Sour Soup

Meaty mushrooms and sherry cooking wine give this soup plenty of delicious flavor to add a highlight to any soup cleanse. Apple cider vinegar and ginger only serve to bring more healthful benefits to the table as well!

Raw grated ginger is packed full of gingerol, a naturally occurring substance that makes ginger the perfect combatant against inflammation as well as indigestion.

Servings: 4

Ingredients:

1 oz dried mushrooms of your choice

8 cups water

3 tbsp cooking sherry

¼ cup apple cider vinegar

2 tbsp low sodium soy sauce

1 ½ tsp salt

1 tbsp fresh grated ginger

1 lb cubed firm tofu

2 tbsp cornstarch

6 sliced scallions

¼ tsp white pepper

Method:

Cover your dried mushrooms with 2 cups of boiling water in a large bowl. Place a dish over the bowl to cover it. Allow them to rehydrate for 30 minutes.

Once reconstituted, drain off the water from the mushrooms, setting them aside for later use. Thinly slice the mushrooms.

In a large soup pot, add the last 6 cups of water as well as the water from the mushrooms. Add in the mushrooms, and heat this mixture over medium-high heat.

Once the ingredients begin to come to a boil, turn the heat down to a simmer, and add in the apple cider vinegar, cooking sherry, salt, ginger, soy sauce and tofu. Simmer for 10 minutes.

While the soup simmers, take a mixing bowl and pour in the cornstarch. Slowly mix in ¾ cup of the soup liquid from the soup pot, while stirring to prevent the cornstarch from becoming lumpy.

When the cornstarch is dissolved, pour it slowly in to the soup pot while stirring. This will thicken the soup.

Add in the white pepper and scallions, and allow to heat for another couple of minutes before serving.

Lunch Soup

Leek and Radish Soup

The less commonly used leek and radish bring a unique flavor combination to this cleansing soup. A milk base gives this soup a creamy texture, which adds more variety to a mostly clear-soup based cleanse.

Fiber-rich radishes are widely known for their toxin purging properties, as well as their cleansing effect on the digestive system.

Servings: 4

Ingredients:

¾ lb halved radishes

3 peeled and cubed potatoes

2 washed and sliced leeks

32 oz low sodium chicken broth

1 tsp sea kelp seasoning

2 tbsp unsalted butter

1 cup milk (whole is best for a creamier soup)

Salt and pepper to taste

Method:

In a large soup pot, melt the butter over medium-high heat. Add the radishes, potatoes and sea kelp seasoning.

Use a large spoon to mix together the ingredients, then slowly pour in the chicken broth. Mix together, then stand your leek leaves in the pot.

Once the soup has come to a boil, reduce the heat, and allow the soup to simmer for around an hour or until the potatoes are fork-tender.

Once the potatoes are fork-tender, remove the leeks from the pot and throw away. Use an immersion blender to mix together the soup in to a creamy consistency.

Add in the milk, mix thoroughly, and add salt and pepper to taste.

Afternoon Soup

Kale and Lentil Soup

Kale and lentil soup is a vegan-friendly filling soup that is guaranteed not to leave you hungry. Ideal for any time of year, this soup is one of the more solid recipes for an entrée soup.

Red lentils provide plenty of protein, leaving you with energy to last through the day. In addition to energy, red lentils also offer cholesterol reduction properties and improved digestion and heart health!

Servings: 4

Ingredients:

8 cups vegetable broth

1 ½ cups rinsed red lentils

2 chopped carrots

2 diced yellow onions

1 bunch chopped kale with stems removed

1 garlic clove, minced

¼ tsp red pepper flakes

1 tbsp chopped parsley

Zest of ½ lemon

Method:

In a large soup pot over medium-high heat, combine the vegetable broth, carrots, lentils, kale, onions and garlic. Stir to mix your ingredients thoroughly.

Bring the soup to a boil, and reduce the heat slightly to allow the soup to simmer while the lentils cook.

When the lentils are tender, add in the lemon zest, red pepper flakes and parsley.

Stir and serve!

Dinner Soup

Green Detox Soup

More greens than you can imagine come together to make this one powerful vegan detox soup with plenty of flavor!

Combining the anti-inflammatory properties of celery with the energy boosting, cholesterol-reducing, heavy metal detoxing properties of garlic, makes this soup a must have if you are serious about getting healthy.

Servings: 14

Ingredients:

1lb chopped green beans

8 chopped celery sticks

4lb chopped zucchini

2 bunches fresh spinach

1 chopped onion

5 fresh chopped garlic cloves

1 bunch chopped fresh basil

1 bunch chopped fresh parsley

Method:

Steam the celery, zucchini and green beans in a pot on your stove until they are soft but do not lose color. If you use a vegetable steamer, you will need to make a few adjustments to your cooking method.

Add the spinach, onion and garlic to the steamer, and cook for another 5 minutes.

Add the basil and parsley, and use a handheld blender to puree the ingredients until you get a soup consistency.

Season with salt and pepper as desired and serve.

Evening Soup

Apple and Butternut Squash Soup

Delicious sweet Gala apples combine with apple juice and butternut squash to make the perfect sweet, yet warming dessert soup for a cold winter night!

Combining the phytonutrients and antioxidant properties of sweet Gala apples with the high levels of B6 found in butternut squash, this soup packs a punch for protecting your nervous system and your immune system.

Servings: 8

Ingredients:

1 butternut squash (2lbs) cubed

4 cubed Gala apples

8 oz halved mushrooms (your choice)

4 stalks largely chopped celery

1 large onion quartered

¼ cup olive oil

4 cups vegetable broth

1 cup apple juice

2 tsp salt

1 tsp pepper

½ tsp ground nutmeg

1 tsp cinnamon

Method:

Preheat the oven to 425°F.

Combine butternut squash, 1/8 cup olive oil and the onion in a bowl and mix together to coat. Put the coated vegetables into a baking pan, and bake in preheated oven for 45 minutes or until fork tender.

While the vegetables are cooking, combine the remaining olive oil with the mushrooms and apples.

Mix together to coat, and spread on a new baking pan. Bake for 20 minutes until soft.

Once the vegetables and fruits are cooked, add them to a soup pot with the vegetable broth and apple juice. Puree this mixture using a hand blender. You may need to add more broth if you want a thinner soup. When blended, simmer on medium-low until heated through. Season with the spices, and stir before serving.

As you can see, the average one day cleanse consists of quite a lot of soup! Six soup meals a day provide plenty of whole nutrition and all of the benefits of whole vegetables and herbs in the process. One of the best ways to plan out a one day soup cleanse like this is to ensure that you begin and end your menu for the day with a sweeter soup.

This plan helps to curb any sweet tooth that you may have without tempting you to cheat yourself out of any progress you have already made in your detox plan. Of course, if you find yourself with a strong sweet tooth at any other point during the day, substitute one of your sweeter soup recipes for one of your savory ones!

CHAPTER 3

Sweet Soup Cleanse Recipes

In this chapter we are going to take a look at some of our favorite sweet soup cleanse recipes. These sweet flavored soups are a great addition to any soup detox because they help to combat the sweet tooth that comes from a lack of unhealthy refined sugars! We suggest implementing these soups for your morning soup serving as well as for your last soup serving of the day.

Cinnamon Apple and Sweet Potato Soup

Cinnamon apples and sweet potatoes make this comforting cleansing soup a great warm start for any sweet breakfast lover!

Cinnamon is packed full of cinnamaldehyde, a naturally occurring substance that provides anti-inflammatory properties, has an anti-diabetic effect and can protect you from bacterial and fungal infections.

Servings: 4

Ingredients:

1lb peeled and cubed sweet potatoes

2 cored and cubed medium-sized apples with peel

1 tbsp freshly chopped ginger

½ tsp ground cinnamon

1 cup apple cider vinegar

Method:

In a large soup pot on medium-high heat, combine the ingredients. Stir to thoroughly mix them, and allow the contents of the pot to come to a boil.

Once boiling, reduce the heat to a simmer, and allow the soup to cook for 30 minutes or until the apples and sweet potatoes are fork-tender.

Remove the soup from the stovetop and allow it to cool down. Once the soup is no longer hot but warm, use an immersion blender to puree the soup until you get a smooth consistency. Serve.

Sweet Corn Soup

This sweet corn soup is a hearty recipe that makes use of fresh summer produce with fresh corn, green onions and onions. This is a filling soup and a favorite for detoxers and their families!

Although rich in carbs, corn is a great vegetable for catering to digestive health. With both soluble and insoluble fiber, corn helps to prevent the absorption of cholesterol while improving regularity.

Servings: 4

Ingredients:

2 tbsp olive oil

½ chopped onion

2 minced garlic cloves

4 quartered red potatoes

Salt and pepper to taste

3 corn ears worth of fresh corn

2 cups low sodium vegetable broth

2 cups milk

3 chopped green onions

Method:

In a large soup pot, heat the olive oil over medium heat. Once hot, add the garlic and onion and sauté for a couple of minutes before adding the potato. Add salt and pepper to taste, then cover the pot and let steam for 5 minutes.

Add the corn to the pot, then add the vegetable broth and milk. Stir to combine, cover and allow to come to a boil. Once boiling, turn the heat to low, and cook until the potatoes are cooked through.

Using an immersion blender, create a smooth consistency to the soup. Taste and season with salt and pepper if needed. Serve hot with the green onion on top.

Chickpea and Lemon Soup

A bright and flavorful soup, this recipe incorporates fresh lemon tempered with just enough cayenne to give it a kick!

Rich in choline, chickpeas help to maintain cell health which in turn helps to decrease inflammation and improve nerve impulse transmission. Also high in fiber, chickpeas are a great way to improve regularity, and they also aid in digestion.

Servings: 6

Ingredients:

2 tbsp olive oil

2 sliced celery stalks

1 chopped onion

6 chopped garlic cloves

1 tsp cumin

1 tsp coriander

¼ tsp turmeric

1/8 tsp cayenne pepper

6 cups cooked chickpeas

6 cups low-sodium chicken broth

1 tsp salt

Black pepper to taste

2 lemons cut into thirds

1 ½ cups freshly cut cilantro, parsley, dill and mint

Method:

In a large soup pot on medium heat, heat the olive oil. Add in the onion, celery and garlic, and sauté until the onion is clear. Add the coriander, cumin, cayenne pepper and turmeric, and stir while cooking for 30 seconds.

Throw the chickpeas in to the pot, and stir before

adding the broth. Taste the soup, and add salt and pepper to your liking. Bring the contents of the pot to a boil before reducing the heat to a simmer. Simmer for 15 minutes.

Using an immersion blender, blend the soup to get a smooth consistency. Serve while hot with lemon juice squeezed on top. Garnish with fresh herbs.

Spiced Apple Soup

A delicious apple-based soup, this recipe makes the perfect breakfast soup option. A healthier version of cinnamon apple pie filling, this soup is a comforting detox soup to get the day started.

The cinnamon that is plentiful in this recipe is loaded with antioxidants that protect body cells from free radical damage.

Servings: 6

Ingredients:

6 cups water

2 ½ lb cored and diced Pink Lady apples with peel

$^{2/3}$ cup raisins

1 tsp nutmeg

1 ½ tsp cinnamon

¼ tsp ground cloves

½ tsp allspice

Salt

¼ cup honey

2 tbsp fresh lemon juice

1 cup plain yogurt

Method:

In a large saucepan on medium-high heat, combine the water, raisins, apples, honey, spices and a pinch of salt. Bring the ingredients to a boil, cover the pan and simmer for around an hour.

After simmering, remove the pan from the heat and add the yogurt and lemon juice. Stir to combine. Serve hot.

Cold Blueberry Soup

The predominant flavor in this bright purple soup is the sweetness of blueberries. This sweetness is tempered with the acidity of orange and white grape juice. The ingredients combine to make an acidic but mouthwatering soup.

One of the best super fruits there is, blueberries

are rich in phytonutrients whose sole purpose is to protect the brain from damage by toxins in the environment.

Servings: 6

Ingredients:

1 orange, juiced

1 cup white grape juice

2 cups fresh blueberries

1 cup plain organic yogurt

Method:

In a large saucepan, add 1 cup water, the grape juice and orange juice. Bring it to a boil. Stir the boiling mixture for 1 minute.

Add in the blueberries, and stir for another minute before removing the pan from the heat. Let the soup mixture cool before blending to a smooth consistency.

Once pureed, strain the soup and put in the fridge to chill before serving. Once chilled, gently mix in the yogurt and serve.

Apple and Curried Sweet Potato Soup

Less of a breakfast soup and more of a main meal soup, this apple and curried sweet potato soup has its sweetness tempered with bright curry flavor.

Madras curry powder is known for its ability to reduce inflammation while providing pain relief at the same time. In addition, curry powder offers antibacterial properties that help guard intestinal health.

Servings: 4

Ingredients:

3 sweet potatoes

3 tbsp butter

1 chopped onion

2 crushed garlic cloves

1 peeled grated knob 2-inch piece of ginger

¼ tsp grated nutmeg

1 ½ tsp Madras curry powder

Salt and pepper to taste

2 cups low sodium chicken broth

1 ¼ cups no sugar added chunky applesauce

1 tbsp olive oil

1 tbsp apple cider vinegar

1 tbsp chopped cilantro

Method:

Preheat oven to 425°F. While the oven pre-heats, peel the sweet potatoes, and dice them.

Melt the butter in a large soup pot on medium-heat, and sauté the garlic and onions until the onions are clear. Now stir in the nutmeg, ginger and 1 ¼ tsp curry powder. Cook for another minute.

Now turn up the heat to medium-high, and put the diced sweet potatoes, 2 cups of water and chicken broth into the pot. Cover and allow the ingredients to come to a boil.

Once boiling, turn the heat down to a simmer, and stir the applesauce in. Re-cover and let simmer for another 20 minutes until the sweet potatoes are tender.

Using an immersion blender, blend the soup to a smooth consistency. Season with salt and pepper.

Before serving, melt 1 tbsp butter in a skillet, and add in the last ¼ tsp curry powder. Once browned, take off the heat and drizzle over individual bowls of soup before topping with cilantro.

Black Sesame Milk Soup

This Chinese soup combines black sesame seeds and long grain rice to create a unique sweet flavor with a delicious rich depth to it.

Packed with protein, black sesame seeds protect DNA against radiation damage, protect the liver from alcohol damage and promote a healthy respiratory tract.

Servings: 4

Ingredients:

1 cup long grain white rice

1 cup black sesame seeds

7 cups water

Method:

Begin by putting the rice in a bowl and covering it with cold water. Allow to soak for 4 hours.

When the rice has soaked long enough, use a skillet and toast the black sesame seeds until they release fragrance. Take the seeds off the heat and pour them on to a plate to cool.

Once your seeds have cooled, drain the water off the

rice, and add the rice to the blender. Pour in 3 cups of water, and puree until smooth.

Pour the pureed rice in to a bowl, and rinse your blender. Now grind the sesame seeds until you get the smoothest texture possible. Add in ½ cup of water, and blend again until smooth.

Use an immersion blender to combine your two mixtures thoroughly.

Pour this combined mixture in to a large soup pot along with 3 ½ cups of water. Bring this pot to a boil over medium-high heat.

Once boiling, turn the heat to low, and simmer for 10 minutes while stirring.

While the soup is simmering, make a pot of boiling water. You are going to use this boiling water to add to the soup to create a smoother texture while blending with your immersion blender. When finished it should resemble honey in thickness and be very smooth.

Serve warm.

Chinese Nut Soup

The smooth nut based soup has a more subtle sweet flavor that comes from the pecans and walnuts.

Packed with liver protecting polyphenols and neuroprotective compounds, walnuts provide brain health, heart protection from aging and have anti-inflammatory properties.

Servings: 4

Ingredients:

½ cup white long grain rice
Water
1 cup mixed toasted walnuts and pecans

Method:

Put the rice into a bowl and cover with enough cold water to just cover the rice. Allow to soak for at least 4 hours.

After the rice is soaked, pour the rice and rice water in to a blender and puree until smooth.

Pour the nuts in to the blender along with 1 cup of water, and puree again until smooth.

Add in more water until you reach the 4 cup mark on the blender, and puree until the soup mix is thoroughly blended.

In a large soup pot on medium-high heat, bring 8 cups of water to a boil. Turn down your heat to medium, and slowly introduce the contents of your blender while stirring the pot. Make sure to scrape the bottom of the pot while stirring to avoid sticking.

Serve warm.

CHAPTER 4

Savory Soup Cleanse Recipes

There are plenty of savory soup recipes to be found for any soup cleanse, but in this chapter we focus on some of the most beneficial. These savory soups provide maximum health benefits in a single bowl!

Homemade Beef Bone Broth Soup

A hearty beef bone broth makes a delicious and nutrient packed base for just about any soup, but it can also be eaten alone. Marrow bones bring a richness to this recipe that just can't be found in store bought broth.

Rich in glycine, marrow bones are great for repairing as well as creating crucial proteins in the body.

Additionally, bone marrow is a good source of elements that the human body requires to purge toxins, but are frequently found in short supply in our everyday diets.

Servings: 4

Ingredients:

4lb mixed beef marrow bones and meaty bones

2 chopped unpeeled carrots

1 cleaned chopped leek

1 quartered onion

1 halved garlic clove

2 chopped celery stalks

2 dry bay leaves

2 tbsp black peppercorns

1 tbsp cider vinegar

Method:

Preheat your oven to 450°F. Lay the leek, carrots, bones, onion and garlic on a baking pan and roast for 20 minutes. Gently stir the vegetables, and cook for another 20 minutes.

In a large soup pot over medium-high heat, add 12 cups water, vinegar, celery, peppercorns and bay leaves. Now carefully scrape the contents of the baking tray in to the pot. The water should be covering the ingredients, and you can add more water if necessary.

Cover the soup pot, and bring to a boil. Once boiling, partially cover the pot, and reduce heat to a low simmer. Let simmer for 8 to 24 hours, occasionally skimming the top.

Take the pot off the stove, and allow to cool a little before straining the soup and throwing away the solid contents.

Serve or allow to cool before chilling. Store in the fridge for up to a week or in the freezer for up to a month.

Chicken Bone Broth and Vegetable Soup

The fresh and nutrient rich bone broth recipe incorporates healthy chicken breast meat with the color and flavor of fresh spinach, carrots and tomatoes.

The collagen found in homemade bone broth is perfect for boosting the immune system, reducing inflammation throughout the body and soothing the digestive tract lining while your body is detoxing.

Servings: 8

Ingredients:

10 cups chicken bone broth (use the above recipe using chicken rather than beef)

1lb cubed chicken breast

1 chopped onion

8 sliced carrots

4 cups chopped baby spinach

2 cups chopped broccoli florets

2 cups stewed tomatoes

½ cup wild rice

Method:

In a large soup pot on medium heat, add all of the ingredients together except for the wild rice. Stir all the ingredients together.

Allow pot to come to a boil, then add the rice and reduce the heat to medium-low. Simmer the soup until all ingredients are cooked through.

Serve hot!

Deep Detox Soup

This bright and colorful soup is packed with flavor and immune boosting properties. Turmeric, cinnamon, garlic and cayenne pepper create a well-seasoned and rich clear cleansing soup.

The addition of turmeric to this recipe makes this soup a great anti-inflammatory without the toxic effects of prescription medications. Combine this with turmeric's ability to improve liver function and this soup is ideal for cleansing.

Servings: 6

Ingredients:

2 tbsp olive oil

¼ cup vegetable broth

½ diced red onion

2 minced garlic cloves

3 diced celery stalks

3 diced carrots

1 chopped head broccoli

1 cup chopped fresh tomatoes

1 tbsp minced fresh ginger

1 tsp turmeric

¼ tsp cinnamon

$1/8$ tsp cayenne pepper

Salt and pepper to taste

6 cups water

2 cups torn kale

1 cup chopped purple cabbage

½ lemon (for juice)

Method:

In a large soup pot on medium-high heat, heat the olive oil and add the garlic and onion. Sauté until your onion is clear, then add the broccoli, celery, carrots, ginger and tomatoes. Cook for 3 minutes while stirring.

Add the cinnamon, cayenne pepper, turmeric and salt and pepper to taste, then stir. Now add the vegetable broth and water and bring to a boil. Once boiling, reduce heat to a simmer. Simmer until the vegetables are tender.

Add the cabbage, kale and lemon juice when the soup is almost finished.

Serve warm.

Creamy Green Soup

Deep green in color, this healthy soup is packed full of green vegetables that are loaded with all of the benefits of greens! A flavorful soup, this recipe incorporates highlights of garlic and the sweetness of bell pepper with earthy spinach.

A whole avocado incorporated in to this recipe makes it a soup full of healthy fats and oleic acid. Oleic plays a significant role reducing inflammation which means that this soup is great for soothing the digestive tract as well as improving overall health.

Servings: 2

Ingredients:

2 cups torn spinach leaves

1 peeled pitted avocado

½ cup sliced cucumber

1 sliced green onion

½ cup chopped red bell pepper

¼ cup vegetable broth

1 minced garlic clove

1 tbsp soy seasoning

1 tbsp fresh lemon juice

A dash of chili powder

Pepper

Method:

Add all of the ingredients in to a blender, and blend until smooth. Once smooth, add to a large saucepan and heat over medium-high until heated through. Serve warm.

Green Potage Soup

Another deep green dish, this hearty soup is packed with protein as well as flavor. Onion, shallots and fresh thyme compliment the sweet peas and temper the flavor of the fresh broccoli.

The high antioxidant levels found in the peas lend their immune system bolstering properties to this thick cleansing soup. In addition, pisumsaponins, a class of anti-inflammatories found in peas, also serve to improve bodily system functioning.

Servings: 4

Ingredients:

1 tbsp olive oil

¼ cup chopped green onions

1 chopped shallot

1 lb broccoli florets

1 tbsp fresh chopped thyme leaves

¼ tsp salt

½ tsp black pepper

3 cups vegetable broth

¾ cup thawed frozen peas

¾ cup cooked green lentils

2 cups torn spinach

Method:

In a large soup pot over medium-high heat, heat the olive oil. Add in the shallots and green onions, and cook for 5 minutes while stirring.

Add the thyme, broccoli and salt and pepper and stir the ingredients. Sauté for another 5 minutes before adding the broth. Bring the soup mix to a boil, then add the lentils and peas.

Cook for 10 minutes or until the vegetables are fork tender. Remove from heat and let cool down to a warm temperature before adding the spinach.

Using an immersion blender, blend the soup until smooth. Add salt and pepper to taste, and serve warm.

Deep Green Detox Soup

If you are looking for a lot of flavor in your detox soup cleanse, this spice filled green detox soup is for you. Garlic, ginger, cumin, cardamom and mint bring a harmonious and refreshing flavor of earthy spices to this dish.

Rich in digestion improving compounds, the cumin in this recipe has benefits that range from improving blood flow to boosting the immune system through antioxidant power.

Servings: 2

Ingredients:

4 chopped celery stalks

1 chopped onion

1 chopped green bell pepper

5 handfuls of spinach rinsed

2 minced garlic cloves

½ tsp cardamom

½ tsp ground ginger

½ tsp ground cumin

1 tsp dried mint

4 ¼ cups water

Salt and pepper to taste

Method:

Over medium-high heat, put the salt and water into a large soup pot, and bring to a boil.

Once boiled, add the celery, bell pepper, onion and spinach to the pot and cover, reducing the heat to medium. Cook until the vegetables are tender.

Remove the pot from the heat and add the garlic, then use an immersion blender to blend the soup into a smooth consistency. Season to taste, and serve warm.

Detoxing Chicken Soup

A savory and hearty soup, this detoxing chicken soup incorporates everything you love about chicken soup with the chunkiness of a vegetable soup.

A great source of lean protein, chicken promotes central nervous system, kidney and liver functioning through its rich phosphorus content.

Servings: 8

Ingredients:

1 ½ lb chicken breast

8 cups chicken broth

1 chopped onion

3 cups chopped broccoli florets

2 ½ cups sliced carrots

2 cups sliced celery

1 ½ cups fresh chopped parsley

4 minced garlic cloves

3 tbsp fresh grated ginger

2 tbsp olive oil

1 tbsp apple cider vinegar

½ tsp crushed red pepper

¼ tsp ground turmeric

Salt and pepper to taste

Method:

In a large soup pot on medium heat, heat the olive oil. Add celery, garlic, onions and ginger, and sauté until the onions are clear. Add in the chicken breasts, carrots, broth, red pepper, vinegar, 1 teaspoon salt and turmeric. Stir, then bring to a boil.

Lower the heat to a simmer, and let simmer for 20 minutes. When the chicken is cooked through, take it out and set it aside.

Add the parsley, broccoli and peas to the soup pot and simmer until the broccoli is tender.

Shred the cooked chicken, add it back to the pot and stir.

Season with salt and pepper to taste, and serve warm.

Arugula and Broccoli Soup

A thin green soup, this arugula and broccoli soup has a simple flavor with the depth of the broccoli highlighted by citrus tones or fresh lemon.

The tender arugula leaves in this cleansing soup recipe offer nitrate supplementation that provides improved oxygenation of the body. With more oxygen, the body has a better recovery time and increased energy levels.

Servings: 2

Ingredients:

1 tbsp olive oil

1 sliced garlic clove

½ diced onion

2/3 lb broccoli florets

2 ½ cups water

¼ tsp salt

¼ tsp black pepper

¾ cup arugula

½ lemon

Method:

In a large saucepan over medium heat, heat the olive oil. Once hot, add in the onion and garlic, and sauté until soft.

Add in the broccoli, and cook for 4 minutes before adding salt, pepper and water to the pot. Let the pot ingredients come to a boil, then cover the pot and reduce the heat to a simmer. Cook until the broccoli is fork tender.

Use an immersion blender to give the soup a smooth consistency. Add in the arugula, and blend again to combine.

Serve warm with a slice of lemon on the side.

Collard Green Soup

The earthy flavor of mustard greens and collard greens is highlighted with fresh ginger in this simple, but nutritious green soup recipe.

The combination of antioxidants and sulfur nutrients in collard greens offer extreme detox benefits. These elements work to support the body's own detox system so that they can efficiently do their job.

Servings: 4

Ingredients:

12 cups low-sodium vegetable broth

2 cups chopped mustard greens

2 cups chopped collard greens

1 chopped onion

2 tbsp low sodium soy sauce

2 tsp chopped fresh ginger

Salt and pepper to taste

Method:

In a large soup pot on high heat, add all of the ingredients, and stir to combine. Bring to a boil. Once boiling, cover the pot and reduce heat to a simmer for 30 minutes.

When the vegetables are tender, use an immersion blender to create a smooth soup. Add salt and pepper to taste, and serve warm.

CHAPTER 5

Vegan Soup Cleanse Recipes

Vegan and vegetarian soups are ideal for detoxing as they contain no saturated fat and provide whole body cleansing and detoxification. These soups make for great lunches and even mid-day snacks. Cook a large pot on Sunday and use them throughout the week as palate cleansers.

Detox Vegetable Soup

This thick and hearty vegetable based soup is almost a stew. Packed chock full of nutrient-rich vegetables, this soup not only cleanses, but it also satisfies the hunger for something a little more solid during your detox cleanse.

Protection against cancer, reduction of cholesterol and improved satiety are just a few benefits that come from eating cabbage. Equally as important for the detoxer, however, is the ability of cabbage to improve your body's resistance to infection.

Servings: 6

Ingredients:

1 tbsp olive oil

½ chopped cabbage head

1 can (28 oz.) chopped tomatoes undrained

½ cup tomato paste

1 ½ cups dry lentils

2 cups cooked kidney beans

4 peeled sliced carrots

2 sliced celery stalks

1 chopped red pepper

1 container sliced mushrooms

1 chopped yellow onion

4 crushed garlic cloves

Pepper to taste

3 sprigs fresh basil

Water

Method:

Add your olive oil to the bottom of a large soup pot, and heat on medium-high until hot. When hot, add onions and garlic, and stir while cooking for 1 minute.

Add in the cabbage, and allow to cook while stirring for another minute before adding in the celery, carrots, red pepper, tomatoes, tomato paste, beans, lentils, water and seasoning. Stir to combine the ingredients well. Allow these ingredients to come to a boil before reducing heat to a simmer.

Let the soup simmer for 20 – 30 minutes before adding the mushrooms and covering the pot. Cook for another 90 minutes to 2 hours until the lentils are fully cooked. Serve hot.

Calming Miso Soup

This miso based soup is perfect for healing the whole body while incorporating the earthy flavor of mushrooms and the sweet but spicy highlight of ginger! This is a deep and mellow soup in taste and a rejuvenating soup for every part of your body.

A probiotic food, miso paste has a number of beneficial effects on the digestive system including supporting healthy bacteria colonies. Additionally, miso is known for its ability to chelate and eliminate heavy metals from the body.

Servings: 2

Ingredients:

3 tsp miso paste

1 medium knob of ginger grated

2 minced garlic cloves

½ red onion sliced

1 peeled thinly sliced carrot

1 cup broccoli florets chopped

6 quartered button mushrooms

1 cup baby leaf spinach roughly chopped

1 seeded and finely chopped chili pepper of your choice

2 finely chopped spring onions (not scallions)

Method:

Add 4 cups of water to a large saucepan, and add the miso paste. Heat on low heat to a near boil.

Remove pan from the heat just before the ingredients reach their boiling point, and add in the ginger, garlic, red onion, carrot, broccoli, mushrooms, spinach and chili. Stir to combine.

Spoon in to individual bowls and serve warm, topped with green onion.

Coconut and Lemongrass Soup

This coconut milk based soup is creamy and filling, but the addition of chili paste adds a kick of heat without being too much to handle. Add a touch of lemongrass and some sweet basil and there is just enough sweetness to perfectly round out this flavor profile.

Packed with vitamins B1, B3, B5, B6, C, E, iron, calcium, selenium, phosphorus and magnesium, it's no wonder that coconut milk is so nourishing to the body. With plenty of electrolytes to fight fatigue and nourish the digestive system, coconut milk is the perfect calming ingredient to include in your soup cleanse.

Servings: 4

Ingredients:

2 cans light coconut milk

1 cup water

2 zucchinis cut in to ribbons (use vegetable peeler to cut)

1 container button mushrooms

4 crushed fresh garlic cloves

3 blades fresh lemongrass

2 chopped bunches sweet basil

1-inch knob ginger grated

1 tbsp dry chili paste

1 tbsp red pepper flakes

Soy sauce

Salt and pepper to taste

Method:

Add a tablespoon of dry chili paste to a large saucepan over medium heat, and heat until fragrant.

In a blender, combine the lemongrass, ginger, garlic, two cans coconut milk and 1 cup water. Puree until smooth, then add to the saucepan with the chili paste.

Bring the soup to a boil as you sauté the mushrooms in soy sauce in a small skillet.

Taste the soup, and add salt if needed.

Now add the mushrooms, zucchini and red pepper to the soup, and stir. Serve in small bowls topped with the sweet basil leaves.

Zucchini Soup

A beautiful bright green soup, this zucchini soup is highlighted with fresh garlic, fresh dill and some coconut milk for texture. Ideal for those warm summer days, this fresh soup flavor is a great snacking soup for smaller meals during the day.

A great source of fiber, copper, phosphorus, magnesium, potassium and vitamin A, zucchini is not only healthy, but it is also hydrating as well. Low in calories and great for fighting the effects of too much sodium, zucchini makes this soup great for combating bloating.

Servings: 4

Ingredients:

¼ cup diced onion

1 chopped fresh garlic clove

3 whole dill stems

½ cup vegetable broth

Salt and pepper to taste

4 cups diced zucchini

2 tbsp freshly cut dill fronds

¼ cup coconut milk

Method:

In a large saucepan over medium heat, combine the vegetable broth, garlic, dill stems and onion. Add a dash of salt and pepper. Stir to combine the ingredients, and bring to a simmer.

Allow the soup mixture to simmer for 5 minutes before adding in the squash. Cook for another 10 minutes until the squash is fork tender.

Remove the dill stems before adding in the dill fronds to the soup. Use an immersion blender to give the soup a smooth consistency.

Add the coconut milk, and blend again to mix. Taste to see if you need more salt and pepper. Serve warm.

Cauliflower and Curry Soup

This cauliflower and curry soup elevates the earthy flavor of cauliflower with green curry and coconut milk. A creamy, yet vegetable packed soup, this hearty recipe is the perfect way to incorporate some lesser known, but stellar ingredients in to your whole body detox.

Green Thai chilies in Thai green curry paste are filled with capsicum – the substance responsible for that spicy kick! Capsicum is a great anti-inflammatory and analgesic and its incorporation in this recipe makes this soup perfect for healing the whole body.

Servings: 6

Ingredients:

2 tbsp olive oil

1 cup washed and chopped leeks

$1/3$ cup chopped fresh cilantro

1 ½ lb cauliflower florets

1 tbsp basmati rice

Salt to taste

2 tbsp Thai green curry paste

1 tbsp lemongrass paste

1 knob peeled grated fresh ginger

1 can coconut milk

2 ¼ cups vegetable stock

1 large lime (for juice)

2 tbsp coconut butter

Red pepper flakes to garnish

Method:

Heat the olive oil in a large soup pot on low-medium heat. When heated, add in cilantro, leeks, rice, cauliflower and 1 ½ teaspoon salt. Stir to mix. Cook for 5 minutes, stirring periodically.

In a large mixing bowl, add the grated ginger, green curry paste, lemongrass paste, coconut milk and enough vegetable stock to make 4 cups of liquid including the coconut milk itself. Whisk these ingredients together.

Pour the mixing bowl contents over the soup pot contents, and turn up the heat to high. Once the pot is boiling, turn the heat down to a simmer, and partially cover the pot.

After 25 minutes, or when the cauliflower is tender, remove the pot from the heat. Allow to cool for a few minutes before using an immersion blender to create a smooth soup.

Return the pot to the stovetop, and add lime juice and season to taste with salt and pepper.

Serve warm, stirring in the coconut butter just before serving.

Butternut Squash and Coconut Soup

This beautiful autumn-themed soup is a creamy based soup flavored with smoked paprika and coriander.

Creating a deep and smoky flavor, the ingredients of this thick soup really harmonize well for a hunger fighting soup cleanse recipe.

High in fiber, potassium and vitamin A, butternut squash has more than a few great health benefits. One of the most appealing for soup cleansers, is the ability of butternut squash to improve overall immune function through high doses of beta carotene and vitamin C.

Servings: 3

Ingredients:

2 tbsp olive oil

1 diced onion

2 peeled minced garlic cloves

2 cups diced butternut squash

½ tsp smoked paprika

2 ¼ cups vegetable stock

Black pepper to taste

½ cup dry red lentils

5 oz. coconut milk

1tbsp chopped fresh coriander

Method:

Heat the olive oil over medium-heat in a large saucepan. Once heated, add in the garlic, squash and onion, and cook until the onion is tender.

Add the paprika to the pot and stir, cooking for a minute before adding the vegetable stock. Add a little black pepper to taste, and allow the pot contents to come to a simmer.

In a separate saucepan, cook the lentils until they are soft.

When the squash is fork tender, use an immersion blender to make the soup smooth before adding the coconut milk. Allow the soup contents to come back up to medium-heat.

Once the soup is hot and the lentils soft, add the lentils to serving bowls and cover with the soup. Garnish with chopped coriander and serve.

Roasted Carrot Soup

A truly beautiful soup to look at, this thick orange soup is a sweet vegetable soup with savory ginger highlights. Not your traditional soup, this carrot rich recipe is light but satisfying.

Rich in beta-carotene, carrots help the body to make vitamin A, a vitamin crucial to immune system health as well as vision. Beta-carotene is also known for its ability to fight free radicals and protect the body against the signs of aging.

Servings: 4

Ingredients:

2 lb peeled diced carrots

2 tbsp olive oil

3 tbsp vegan butter

1 diced onion

2 diced celery stalks

2 tbsp grated fresh ginger

4 cups low-sodium vegetable broth

4 cups water

2 tbsp salt

¼ tsp white pepper

Method:

Pre-heat the oven to 425°F, and spread the carrots out on a baking pan. Sprinkle with olive oil and roast for 45 minutes making sure to stir half way through. Take out of the oven when done.

Take a large soup pot and over medium-heat, melt the vegan butter. Add the onions to the pot, and cook until clear, then add in the ginger and celery. Cook for 4 to 5 minutes and then add the carrots, water, vegetable broth, salt and pepper. Stir to combine. Bring to a boil, then reduce heat to simmering. Cover your pot completely, and simmer for 45 minutes.

Using an immersion blender, carefully puree the soup until you get a smooth consistency. Taste and season with salt and pepper to your liking. Serve hot.

CHAPTER 6

Gluten Free Soup Cleanse Recipes

As with vegans, it can sometimes be difficult to find detox programs that are gluten-free. In this chapter we will focus only on gluten free soup cleanse recipes that are designed to help you feel healthier without causing gluten-related problems.

Green Ginger Soup

The warmth of ginger comes together with plenty of fresh greens in this bright green cleansing soup. Packed with more vitamins than you can imagine, this soup is the ideal lunch time pick me up recipe!

Cancer prevention, reduced blood pressure, healthy

skin and hair and diabetes management are just a handful of health benefits offered by spinach.

Servings: 4

Ingredients:

2 tsp coconut oil

2 chopped garlic cloves

2 tbsp chopped onion

1 inch peeled chopped knob of ginger

4 cups chopped fresh broccoli

½ lb fresh spinach leaves

3 peeled chopped parsnips

2 trimmed chopped celery stalks

Small bunch parsley chopped

Water

Salt and Pepper to taste

1 Lemon for juice

Method:

Add the oil to a large soup pot, and heat over medium-heat. Once heated, add the ginger, garlic and onion to the pot. Stir, then add the parsnips, broccoli, spinach, parsley and celery to the oil. Stir to mix and allow to cook just until the spinach wilts.

Once the spinach wilts, add water to the pot until the vegetables are covered. Allow the contents of the pot to come to a high simmer, then reduce the heat to a medium simmer. Cover the pot, and allow the soup to cook until the vegetables are fork tender.

When the vegetables are fork tender, use an immersion blender to puree the ingredients to a smooth consistency. Add salt and pepper and lemon juice to taste. Serve.

Ginger and Pumpkin Soup

Another perfect soup for those cool winter evenings, this ginger pumpkin blended soup is easy and fast to make, and features just six ingredients.

An incredible source of beta-carotene and vitamin A, pumpkin is a great immune system booster. With high levels of antioxidants and vitamin C, pumpkin is also great for the heart.

Servings: 4

Ingredients:

3 cups mashed roasted pumpkin
2 cups gluten-free low sodium chicken stock

¾ cup coconut milk

2 tbsp fresh lemon juice

1 tsp fresh minced ginger

Method:

Add your chicken stock, pumpkin and coconut milk to a blender, and puree them until you get a smooth consistency.

Once a smooth consistency is achieved, add the ginger and lemon juice. Blend once again until the soup is thoroughly mixed.

Pour the ingredients from the blender into a saucepan, and heat on medium-high heat until the soup comes to boil. Once boiling, reduce the heat and allow to simmer for 5 minutes before serving.

Cold Carrot Soup

The highlighting flavor of carrots in this gluten-free soup is only enhanced by the addition of garlic and onion. This sweet cold soup might be your first cold soup adventure, but it sure won't be your last!

Plenty of fiber and incredible levels of beta carotene, make carrots a great power food to add to any soup cleanse routine. Known for its anti-aging properties, beta carotene is also a great anti-cancer agent and antibiotic.

Servings: 4

Ingredients:

2lbs peeled and diced carrots

1 peeled and diced onion

2 peeled and diced garlic cloves

4 cups gluten-free low-sodium vegetable broth

Salt and pepper to taste

Method:

In a large saucepan over medium-high heat, add the vegetable broth, garlic, carrots and onions. Bring to a boil. Allow this mixture to simmer uncovered until the carrots are fork tender.

When the carrots are tender, drain the liquid in to a large bowl or saucepan and add the vegetables to a blender. Puree the vegetables until they are smooth.

Once the vegetables are smooth, add ½ cup of broth and blend. Continue adding ½ cup of broth at a time and mixing the ingredients until you have a soup consistency that suits your preference.

Season the soup to your taste with salt and pepper, and then place your soup in the refrigerator to allow it to chill before serving.

Cauliflower Bacon Soup

The addition of bacon to this delicious soup brings a smoky and delicious highlight that can't be beaten. A delicious and filling soup, this is the perfect soup for detoxing during any time of year.

A part of the cruciferous family, cauliflower is not only rich in antioxidants, but it is also known for its role in fighting inflammation, improving heart health, fighting cancer and detoxifying the body as a whole.

Servings: 4

Ingredients:

6 slices of nitrate-free, gluten-free bacon

1 chopped head cauliflower

4 cups gluten-free low sodium vegetable broth

2 cloves fresh garlic, minced

1 tsp salt

½ tsp black pepper

2 tbsp chopped chives

Method:

Cut the bacon slices in to small pieces before adding to a skillet on medium-heat until cooked through. Once cooked remove from the pan, and set aside.

Now in a large saucepan over high heat, add the vegetable broth, cauliflower, salt, garlic and pepper. Stir to combine the ingredients, and then allow the soup mix to come to a boil.

Once the ingredients come to a boil, reduce the heat to a simmer and cover the saucepan. Allow the soup to simmer until the cauliflower is fork tender.

When the cauliflower is cooked through, add the soup to a blender and puree the ingredients. Then, return the soup to the saucepan and reheat before serving.

Serve in small bowls with a sprinkle of bacon and chives on top as a garnish.

Butternut Squash and Chipotle Soup

Chipotle pepper brings a kick to this thick and creamy soup, highlighting the subtle flavor of butternut squash. A great soup for warming up during winter months or simply adding a little spice to your detox routine.

Cancer prevention isn't the only benefit of eating chipotle peppers. These peppers protect the digestive tract from heart disease, aid in weight loss and reduce blood pressure.

Servings: 5

Ingredients:

2 tbsp olive oil

1 diced yellow onion

2 diced medium carrots

1 2 lb butternut squash peeled, seeded and diced

5 cups gluten-free vegetable broth

1 minced chipotle pepper in adobo

Salt and black pepper to taste

Method:

In a large soup pot over medium-high heat, heat the olive oil. Once heated, throw in the carrots and onions, and sauté until fork tender.

Once the carrots and onions are tender, add in the chipotle pepper, squash and vegetable broth. Stir to combine the ingredients and then allow the soup mixture to come to a boil.

Once boiling, put the lid on the soup pot, and reduce the heat to a simmer. Cook until the squash is fork tender.

Once the squash is tender, carefully pour the soup in to the blender and puree until smooth.

Once pureed, pour the soup back in to the pot and heat before serving. Add salt and pepper to taste.

Shiitake Soup

Meaty shiitake mushrooms add a little more substance to this filling soup. While garlic, shallots and sherry provide plenty of flavor boost. This is most definitely not your ordinary earthy mushroom soup.

The overall immune support offered by shiitake mushrooms has been long documented. From protecting against heart disease to its ability to fight fungi, bacteria and viruses, the shiitake mushroom is an all-around powerhouse.

Servings: 8

Ingredients:

2 oz dry shiitake mushrooms
4 tbsp olive oil

2 bunches sliced green onions

2 minced shallots

4 sprigs thyme

3 minced garlic cloves

1 ½ lbs fresh, cleaned and chopped shiitake mushrooms

1 ½ tsp salt

1 tsp black pepper

¼ cup cooking sherry

2 tbsp gluten-free all-purpose flour

4 cups gluten-free vegetable stock

Method:

Add the dried mushrooms to a large bowl, and cover them with 4 cups of boiling water to allow them to rehydrate. Once rehydrated, scoop the mushrooms from the bowl, and set aside. Now strain the water through a coffee filter in to another bowl, and set aside.

Now take a large soup pot, and heat the olive oil on medium-high heat. Once heated, add all but ½ cup of the green onions to the pot, followed by the garlic, thyme and shallots. Cook until the vegetables are tender.

When the vegetables are tender, remove the sprigs from the thyme. Then add the rehydrated mushrooms and fresh mushrooms to the pot, stirring to combine. Cook until any liquid released from the mushrooms has evaporated.

Add in the sherry, salt and pepper. Stir the ingredients to combine, then cook until the sherry has evaporated.

Add in the flour to the pot, and gently stir to coat everything with the flour. Now, add in the mushroom water as well as the vegetable stock. Allow this mixture to come to a boil before reducing the heat to a simmer. Simmer the pot for 30 minutes.

After 30 minutes, use a blender to puree the soup until you get a smooth consistency. If needed, return the soup to the pot to heat before serving. Serve with the reserved green onions as garnish.

Spinach Lentil Soup

Spinach lentil soup makes for one of the most filling entrée soup recipes there is. This hearty but healthy soup is the perfect option for the "biggest" meal of the day on any soup cleansing menu and is packed with flavor.

High in protein, fiber and plenty of vitamins and minerals, spinach excels in cancer prevention, blood pressure reduction, regulation and overall health of the digestive tract plus bone health.

Servings: 6

Ingredients:

3 crushed garlic cloves

1 diced onion

3 diced large carrots

2 diced celery stalks

2 cups green lentils, rinsed

1 can (14oz.) diced tomatoes undrained

6 cups low-sodium vegetable broth

2 cups water

3 dried bay leaves

½ tsp salt

½ tsp pepper

2 roughly chopped handfuls fresh spinach

Method:

Spray a large soup pot with spray butter (use oil if you prefer), and heat over medium-heat. Once the pot is hot, add in the onions and garlic, and cook until the onions are clear.

Add in celery and carrots, and sauté for another 5

minutes before adding the lentils. Sauté for 5 more minutes after adding the lentils.

Add in the tomatoes with juice, water, bay leaves, vegetable broth and salt and pepper. Stir to combine, and then bring the ingredients to a boil.

Once boiling, cover the pot, and reduce heat to low. Cook for 30 minutes, and then add the spinach. Remove from heat almost immediately, and leave the pot to stand while covered for 2 to 3 minutes to allow the spinach to wilt.

Remove bay leaves before serving.

Hearty Tomato Soup

Delicious and creamy, tomato soup can be just as comforting as it is healthy. Packed with sweet ripened tomatoes, this soup brings plenty of variety in a gluten-free and dairy-free recipe.

Juicy red tomatoes are best known for their ability to fight prostate, colorectal and other cancers, but they also play a role in reducing depression, improving hydration and protecting the heart.

Servings: 6

Ingredients:

1 tbsp olive oil

½ cup diced onion

1 chopped celery stalk

1 peeled chopped carrot

1 chopped garlic clove

1 can (28 oz.) diced tomatoes undrained

1 peeled diced potato

1 ½ cup gluten-free vegetable stock

1 ½ tsp salt

1 tbsp fresh chopped parsley

1 tsp sugar

½ tsp black pepper

Method:

Heat the oil over medium heat in a large soup pot. Once heated, add the carrot, celery, onion and potato to the pot, and cook until fork tender.

Once the vegetables are tender, add in the rest of the ingredients and bring the soup to a boil. Now reduce the heat to a simmer, and continue to simmer for 20 minutes.

After 20 minutes, carefully add the soup to the blender,

and puree until you get a smooth consistency. Serve warm!

Green Asparagus Soup

Although unique in color, this bright green asparagus based soup is refreshing and loaded with nutrients. Unlike other asparagus based soups that can seem watery, this creamy soup is everything you need from a light and satisfying soup.

Asparagus is ideal for flushing toxins such as salt from the body, and its high levels of glutathione aid in breaking down carcinogens and free radicals.

Servings: 4

Ingredients:

6 cups gluten-free low-sodium chicken stock

1 bunch asparagus cut in 2-inch segments

1 quartered yellow onion

3 minced fresh garlic cloves

1 ½ cups frozen garden peas

1 cooked sweet potato

3 tbsp olive oil

¼ tsp white pepper

1 ½ tsp salt

Black pepper to taste

Method:

Heat the oven to 425°F. While pre-heating, heat the chicken stock in a large soup pot. Once boiling, add in the peas, and cover the pot while reducing the heat to simmer.

In a medium mixing bowl, combine the olive oil, onions, garlic and asparagus, and use your hands to mix well. Lay these vegetables on a baking sheet, and sprinkle with salt and pepper. Bake the vegetables for 12 minutes while checking periodically to prevent burning.

Remove cooked vegetables from the oven, and put them in the broth. Remove the inside of the cooked sweet potation, and add to the broth. Use an immersion blender to combine the ingredients in to a thick but creamy consistency.

Sprinkle salt and pepper to taste, and serve warm.

Gluten-Free Hot and Sour Soup

A colorful soup in taste and appearance, this gluten-free hot and sour soup makes for a hearty meal with a delicious and complex flavor profile.

A unique but mild ingredient in this dish, rice vinegar contains plenty of healthy antioxidants that protect against cancer, osteoporosis, heart disease and diabetes.

Servings: 4

Ingredients:

2 tbsp olive oil

1 fresh, minced garlic clove

1 tbsp fresh minced ginger

4 minced scallions

4 cups low sodium, gluten-free chicken stock

1 lb firm tofu

5 cleaned and sliced button mushrooms

1 tsp sugar

2 / 3 cup rice vinegar

3 tbsp low sodium soy sauce

1 tsp black pepper

1 tbsp sesame oil

1 tbsp Sriracha sauce

2 eggs

Method:

Heat the olive oil over medium-high heat in a large soup pot. Add the ginger, garlic and scallions.

After cooking for 1 minute, add the chicken stock. Once simmering, add in the mushrooms, sugar, tofu, soy sauce, vinegar, sesame oil, black pepper and Sriracha. Stir to combine, and bring to a simmer. Once simmering, taste and season more if desired.

While the soup simmers, crack the eggs in to a bowl and whisk. Now whisk the eggs in to your soup, and let the soup come back to simmering.

Portion out the soup, and garnish with green onion. Serve.

Conclusion

Hopefully you have enjoyed learning more about the soup cleansing system as well as flipping through some of our favorite soup cleansing recipes! With forty different detoxifying soups to choose from, you will have enough variety to see you through a number of soup cleanse cycles!

If, however, you find yourself looking for something new after trying each of our recipes, we encourage you to try your hand at creating your own soups! Pick out your favorite flavors and mix them up with some of the more nutritious healing vegetables and herbs and create your own healing combinations.

Remember, don't be afraid to get creative! So long as you taste your soups as you go, you are sure to wind up with a delicious and nutritious meal.

If you enjoyed this book, please leave a review on Amazon.

Be sure to check out our website at
www.thetotalevolution.com for more information.

Thank you!

Preview of 'Bone Broth: The Ultimate Bone Broth Recipes For Wellness And Optimal Health'

Bone broth is not a new trend. Making bone broth is actually an ancient tradition that goes as far back as the early Stone Age period. When our human ancestors were discovering fire and how to make simple tools, their main source of nutrition was animals. They may not have made bone broth like we do today, but they seemed to have had an innate knowledge of the nutritional benefits of bone marrow, as suggested by archeological findings.

It is difficult to pin down exactly when our ancestors first started to boil bones in water and simmer them with plants and herbs, but what we do know is that bone broth soon spread to all parts of the world. Every human culture, in one way or another, soon made this savory broth a staple of their diet. Today, bone broth has become a major ingredient used by many chefs to enhance different types of dishes, due to its rich and complex nature.

Bone broth, also referred to as bone stock, is made

from the bones of grass-fed animals, pasture-raised poultry or pigs, or fish caught in the wild. The bones are slowly simmered in water for many hours so as to extract essential minerals and amino acids. Bones happen to be the most dense and deepest tissues in the body, so in essence you are cooking the root of the animal.

Most of us can still remember the time when we were growing up when bone broth was the go-to food for healing and restoration though we may not have referred to it as such. If you had a tummy ache, grandma made you some soup. If you came down with the flu or had a cold, a steaming mug of chicken soup was always at hand. In fact, by the 19th Century, bone broth, or "invalid beef tea" as it was known then, was primarily viewed as a beverage for people who were sick. Not only was it part of the home diet, but hospital kitchens made it as well.

As the 20th Century rolled in, farming was still widespread, and many small farmers who kept their own animals saw bone broth as a way of maximizing the use of every last piece of carcass. There were different varieties of bone broth made in households, and it was a staple at every meal.

But with urbanization and modernization, traditional

organic bone broth started fading away from most kitchens – until now. In the West, bone broth has come back with a loud bang. However, in the rest of the world, it never went away. In the East, it has always been regarded as a healing beverage that promotes strength, growth of red blood cells and enhances functioning of the liver and kidneys.

For those who have adopted the Paleo diet, drinking bone broth fits right into the Paleo lifestyle. It's important to note that bone broth shouldn't be treated like the superfood du jour or a trend that will be gone tomorrow. It has many nutritious properties that even medical and wellness specialists recognize.

But here's the thing. That store-bought bone broth that comes in a can, box or bouillon cube will not give you the nutrients you need. It may be the easy way to make broth, but it's just full of artificial favors that won't do you any good.

If you truly want to enjoy the numerous and varied healing properties of bone broth, you have to make it the right way. Remember – you cannot substitute organic bone broth made in the traditional way!

Bone broth is much more than just a beverage. It is food that nourishes our digestive system and helps it soak in as many nutrients as possible without using up too much energy. Bone broth is a low-calorie food that builds and maintains our bodies.

So why do we bother boiling bones in water for so long anyway? Well, this slow and lengthy simmering of bones enables all the nutrients in them to be extracted and deposited into the water. In most cases, some type of acid is added (usually apple cider vinegar) in order to maximize the breakdown and extraction of proteins and minerals. This is similar to what our own stomachs acids do.

So what are some of the health benefits of bone broth that wellness advocates, naturopathic physicians, nutritionists, and alternative healthcare providers have been raving about? Here are some reasons why you should eat bone broth:

It repairs your bone tissue and joints.

It improves your nails, skin and hair.

It alleviates acne.

It boosts your fertility and sexual function.

It cures cold and flu.

It helps in weight loss.

It maintains the wellness of expectant mothers.

It strengthens a patient prior to surgery.

It helps the body heal after surgery.

It helps heal wounds and injuries.

It relieves autoimmune diseases such as Crohn's disease and rheumatoid arthritis.

It's plain to see why bone broth is considered good for your overall health. With such a long list of health benefits, it is no wonder that society is now experiencing a bone broth revival.

Bone Broth: The Ultimate Bone Broth Recipes For Wellness And Optimal Health is available for purchase on Amazon.com.

Our Other Books

Below you'll find some of our other books that are popular on Amazon.com and the international sites.

Bone Broth: The Ultimate Bone Broth Recipes For Wellness And Optimal Health

Mayo Clinic Diet: A Proven Diet Plan For Lifelong Weight Loss

Master Cleanse: How To Do A Natural Detox The Right Way And Lose Weight Fast

The Dukan Diet: A High Protein Diet Plan To Lose Weight And Keep It Off For Life

Glycemic Index Diet: A Proven Diet Plan For Weight Loss and Healthy Eating With No Calorie Counting

Clean Eating Diet: A 10 Day Diet Plan To Eat Clean, Lose Weight And Supercharge Your Body

Wheat Belly: The Anti-Diet - A Guide To Gluten Free Eating And A Slimmer Belly

IIFYM: Flexible Dieting - Sculpt The Perfect Body While Eating The Foods You Love

Mediterranean Diet: 101 Ultimate Mediterranean Diet Recipes To Fast Track Your Weight Loss & Help Prevent Disease

Acid Reflux Diet: A Beginner's Guide To Natural Cures And Recipes For Acid Reflux, GERD And Heartburn

Hypothyroidism Diet: Natural Remedies & Foods To Boost Your Energy & Jump Start Your Weight Loss

It Starts With Food: A 30 Day Diet Plan To Reset Your Body, Lose Weight And Become A Healthier You

Made in the USA
Middletown, DE
14 November 2017